Swear Word Coloring Book

SWEAR WORD
ADULT COLORING BOOK
THE VERY RUDE UNDEAD

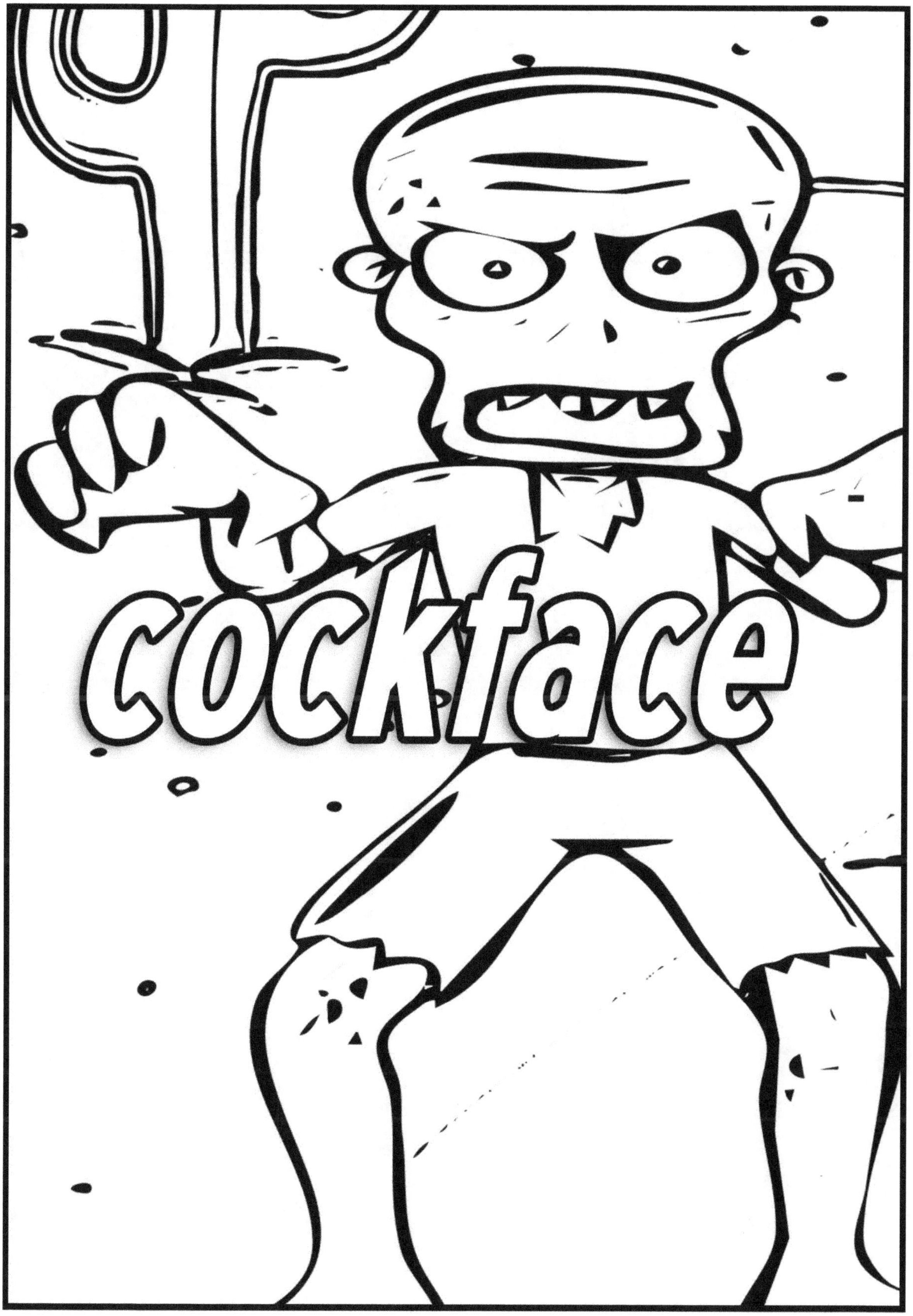
cockface

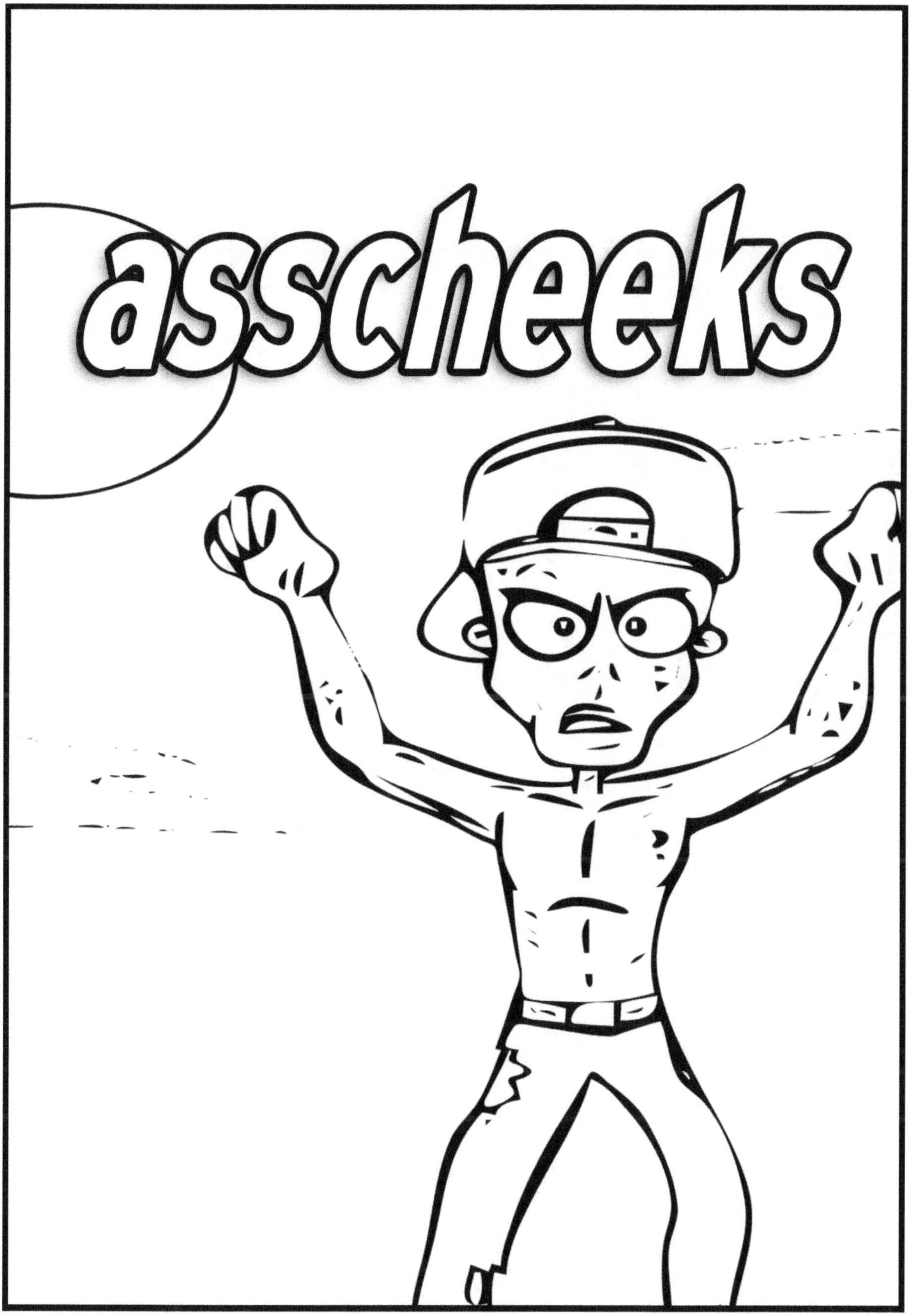
asscheeks

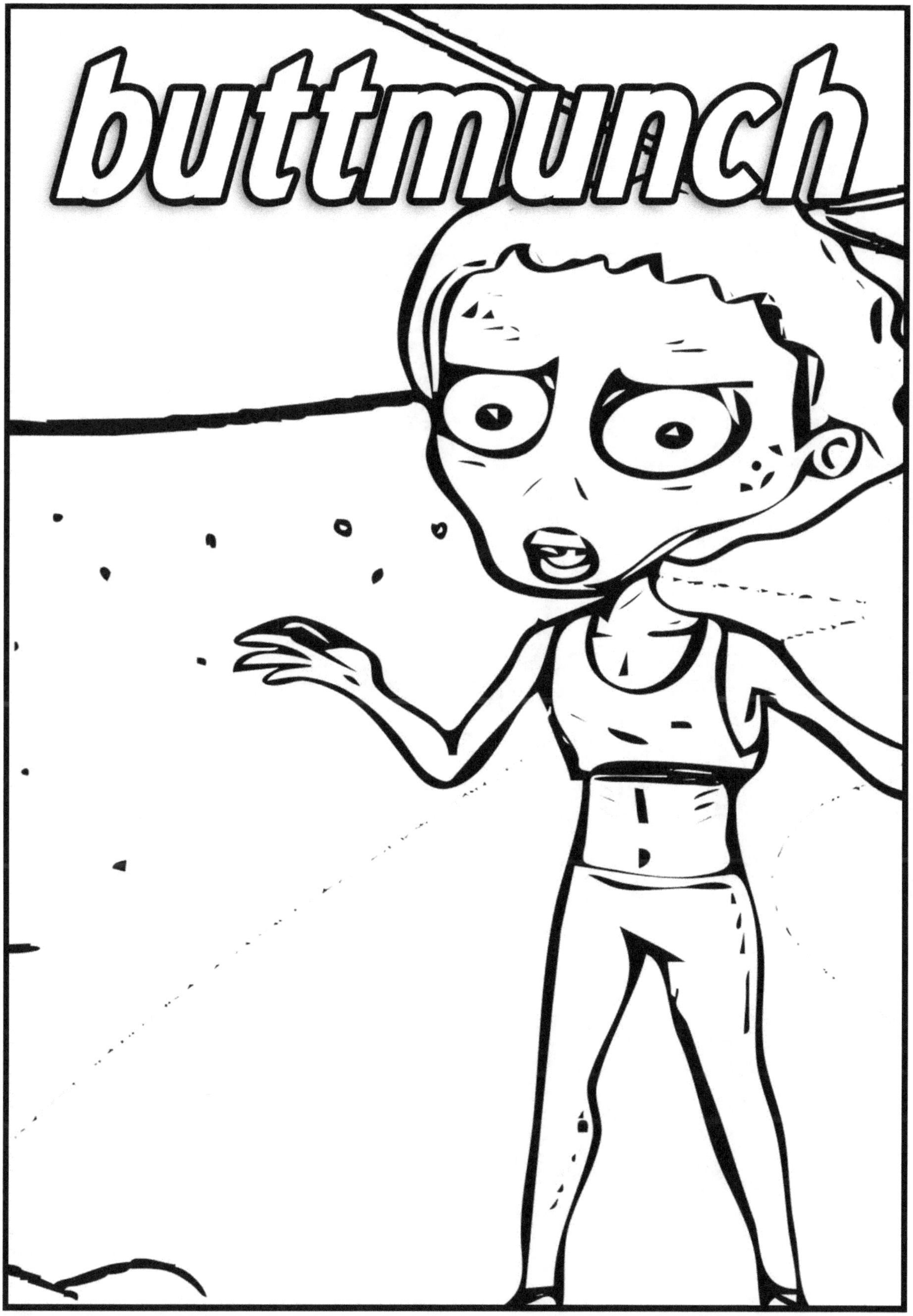
buttmunch

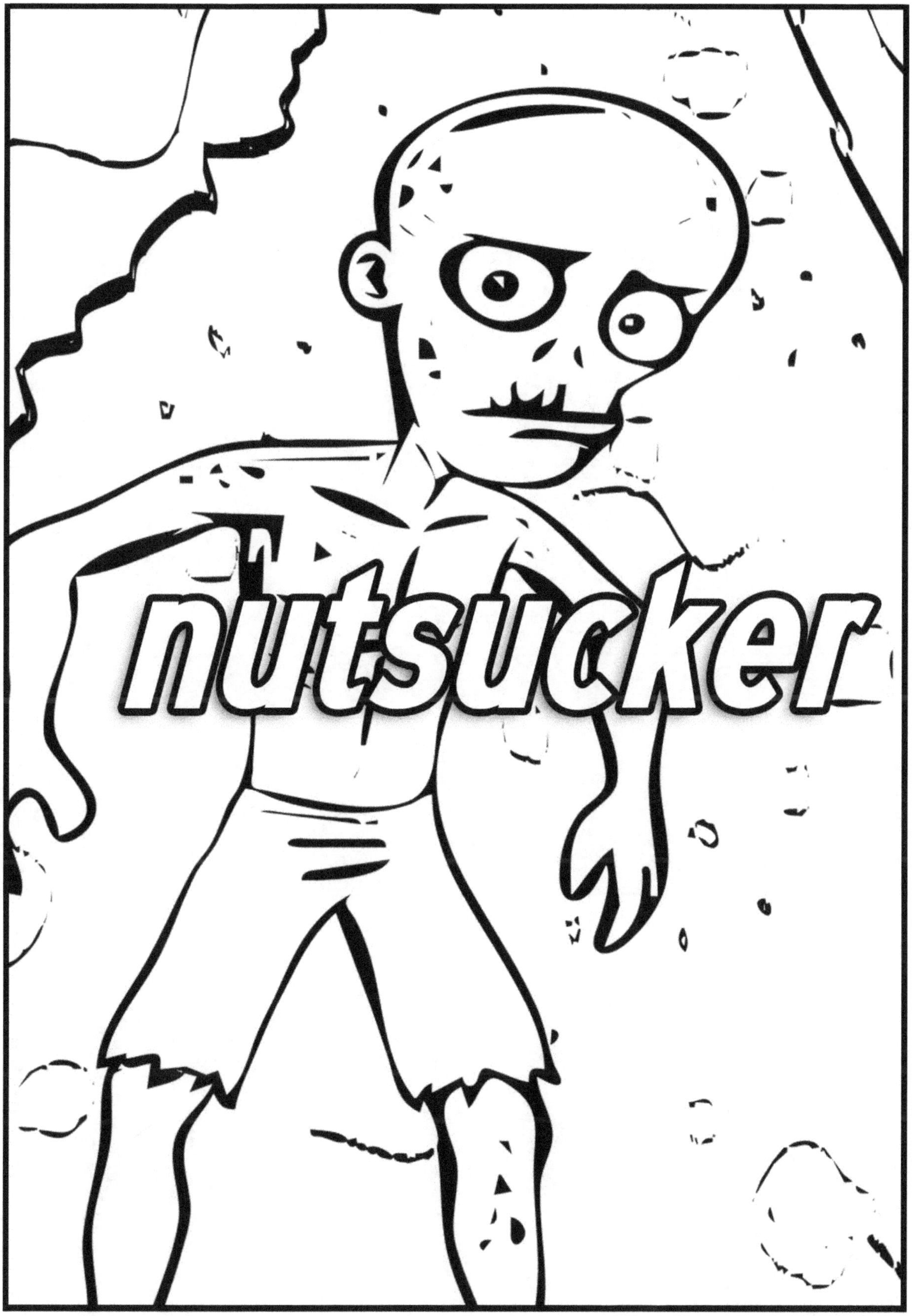
nutsucker

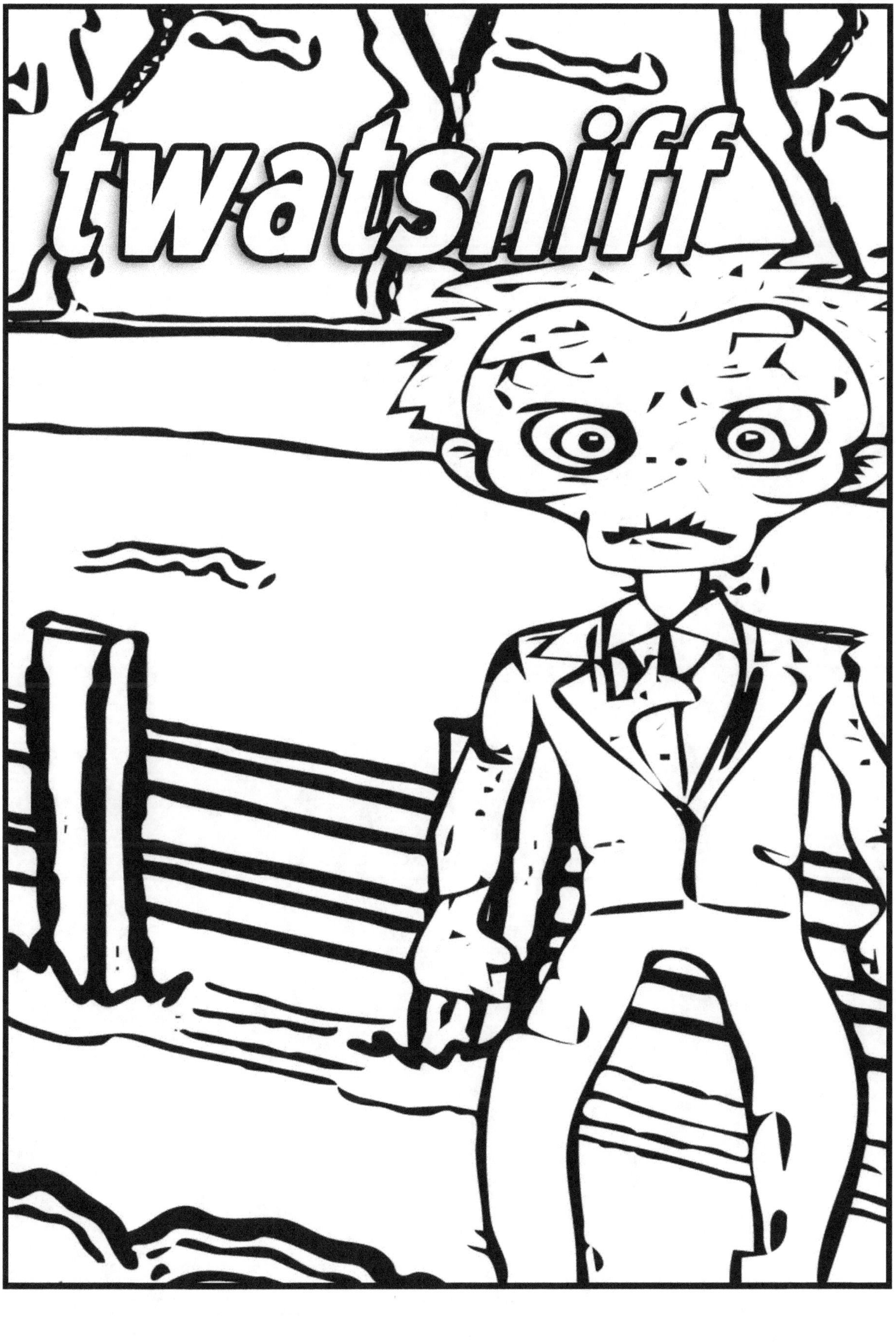
twatsniff

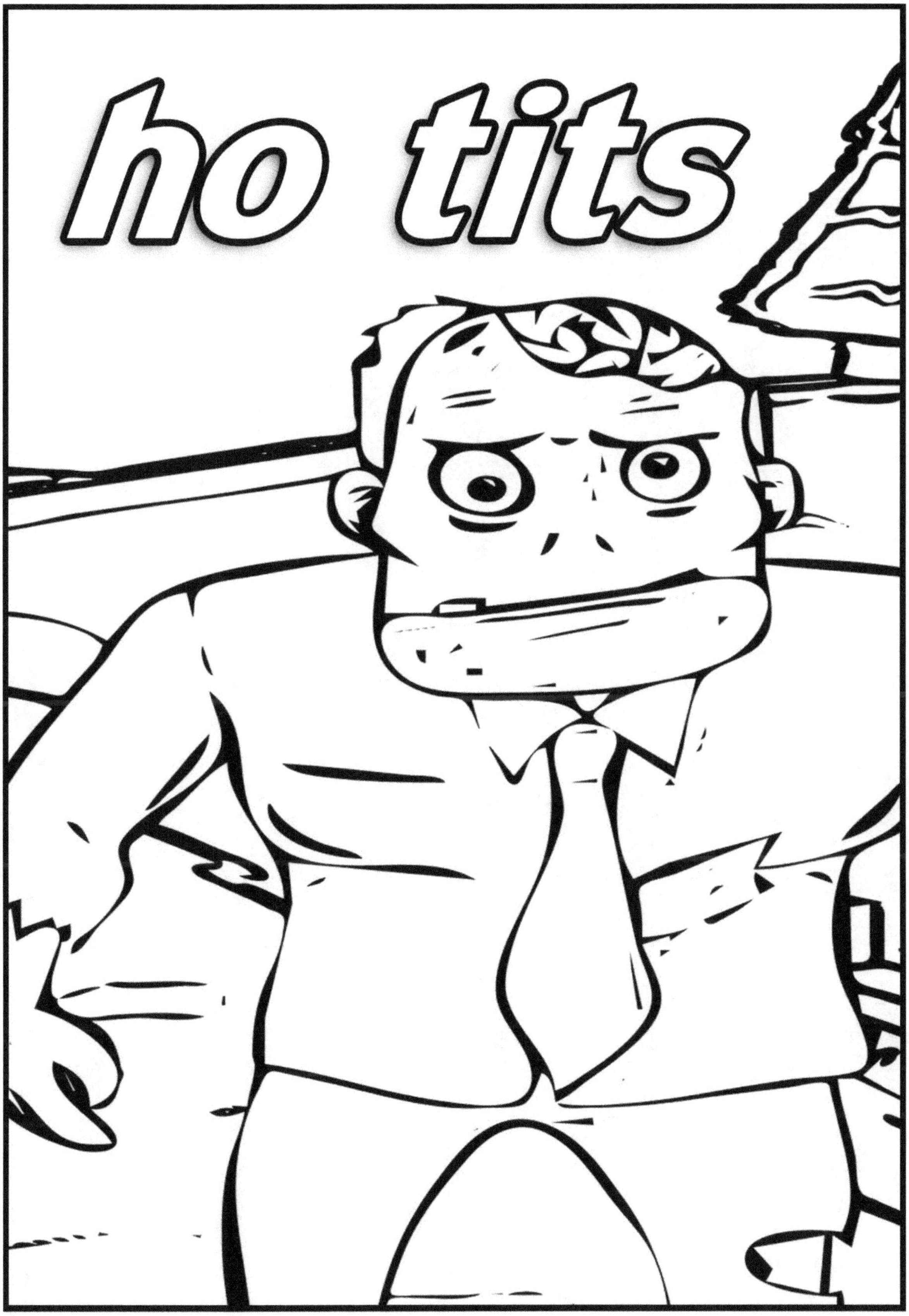
ho tits

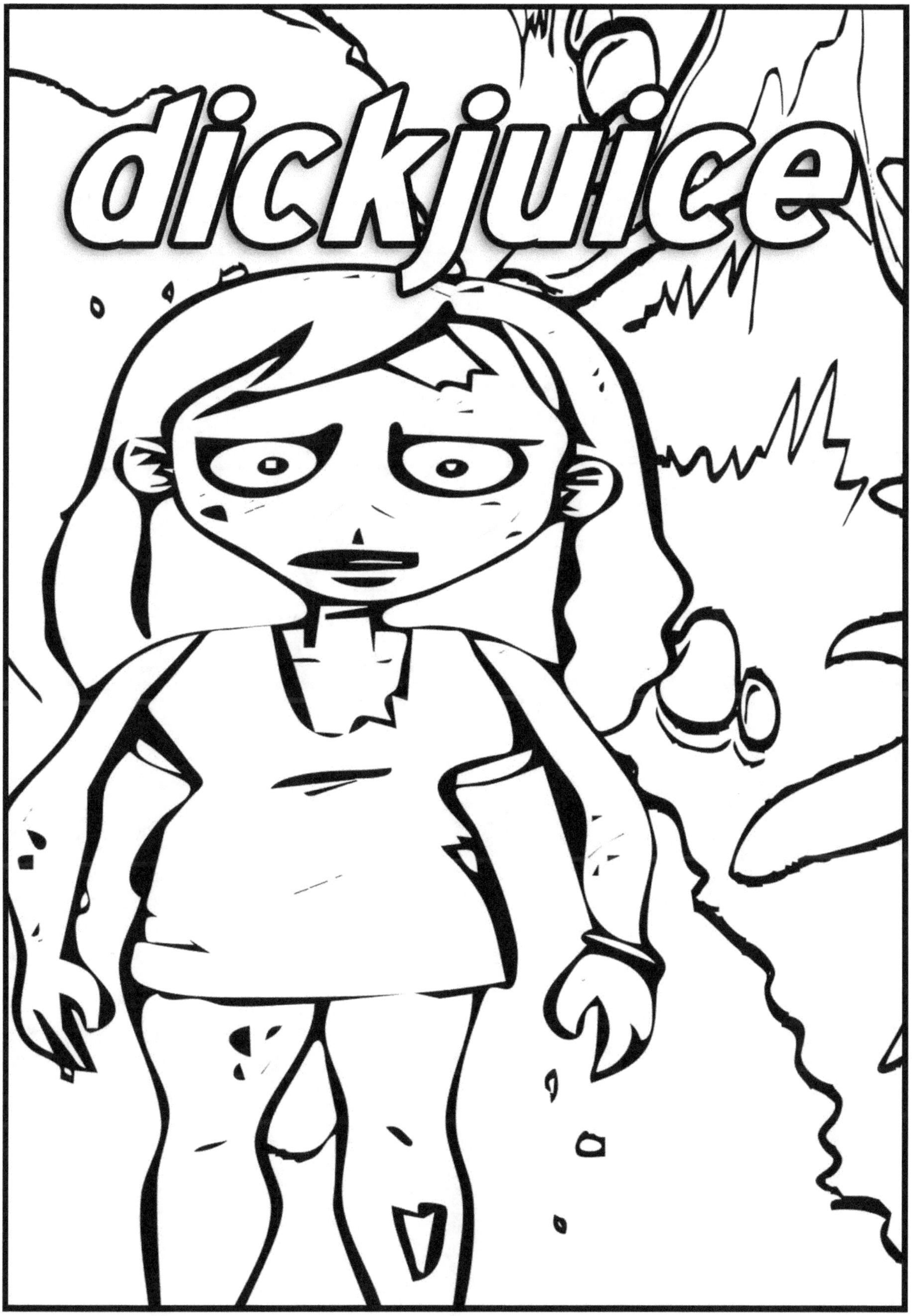
dickjuice

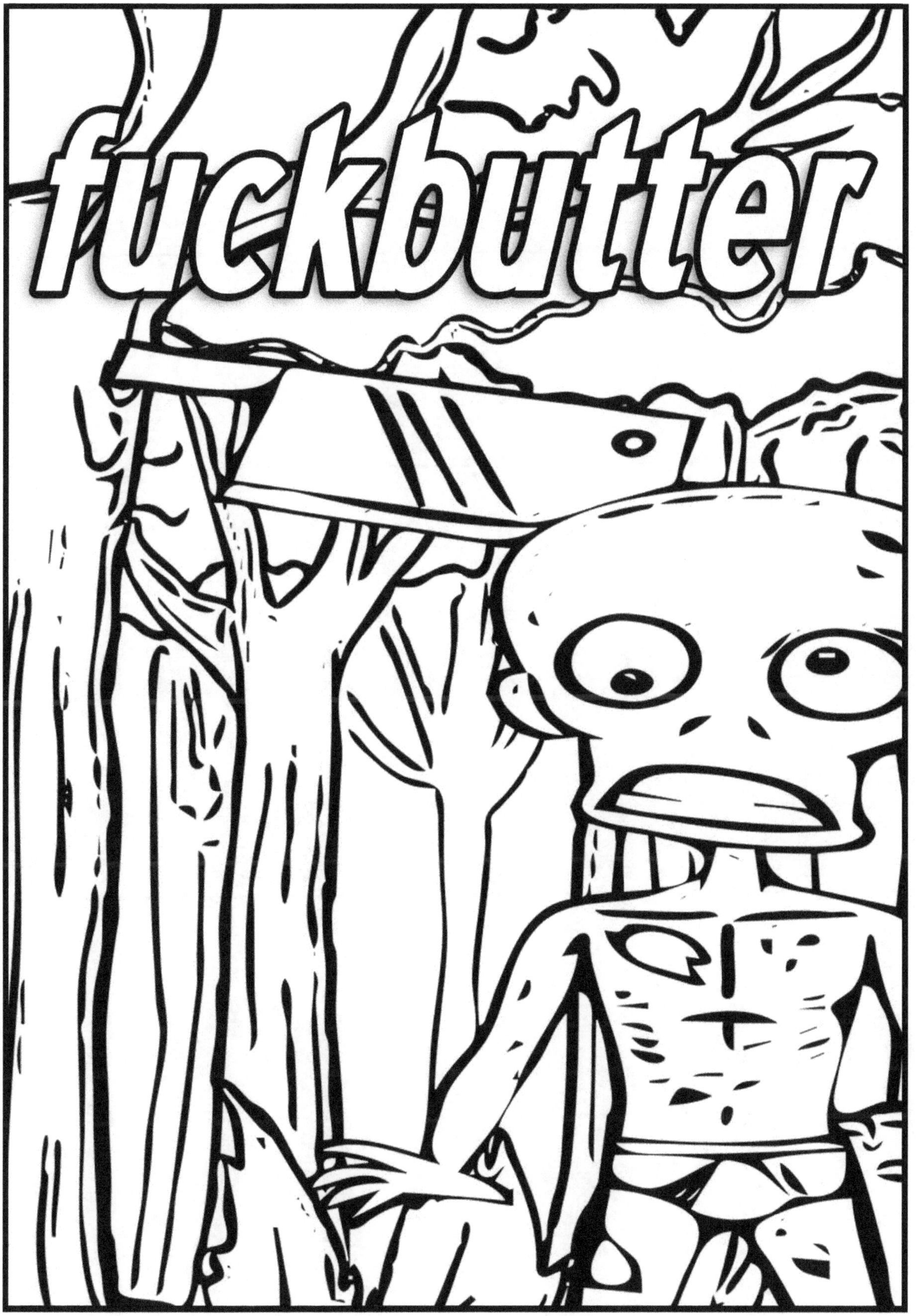
fuckbutter

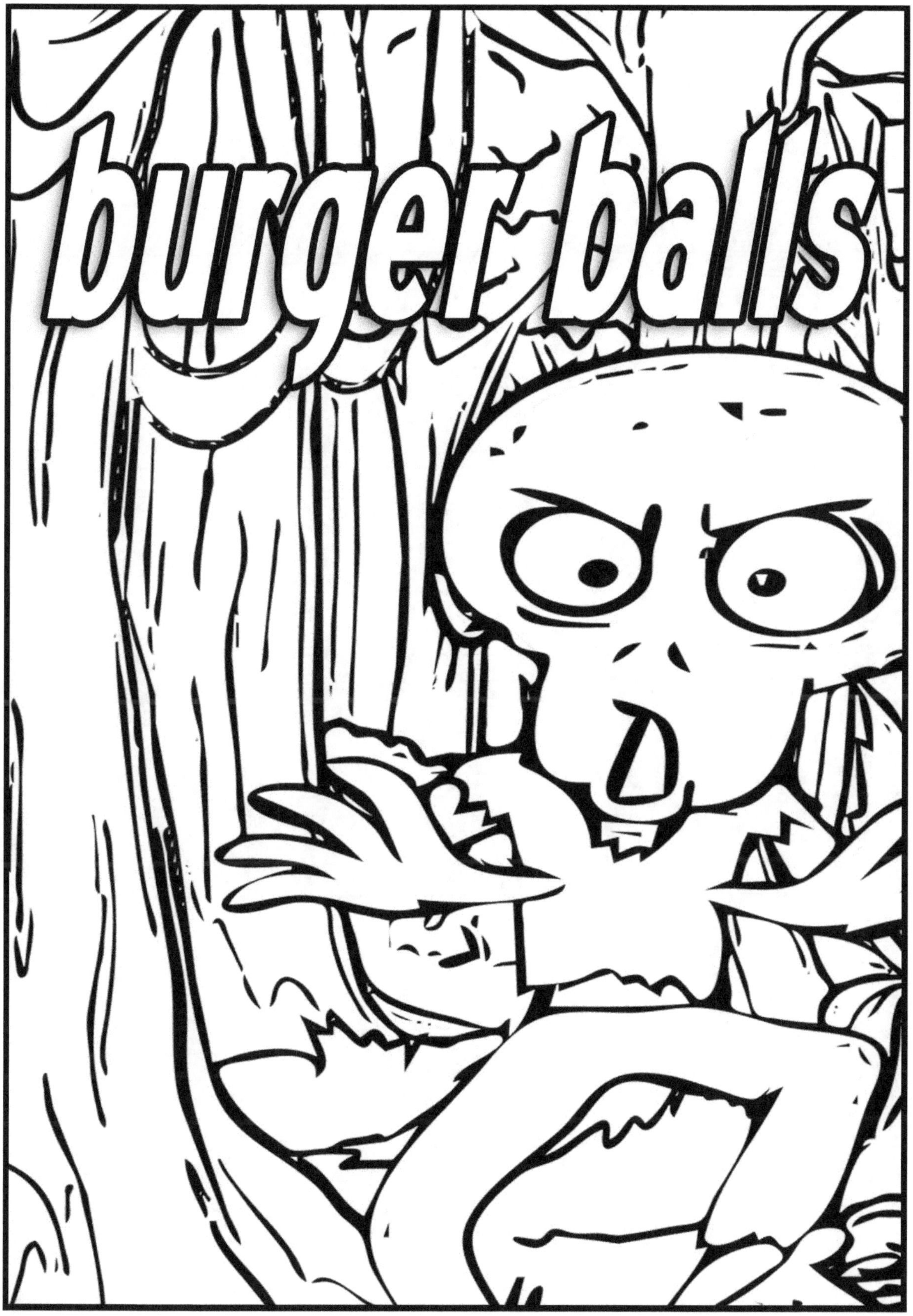
burger balls

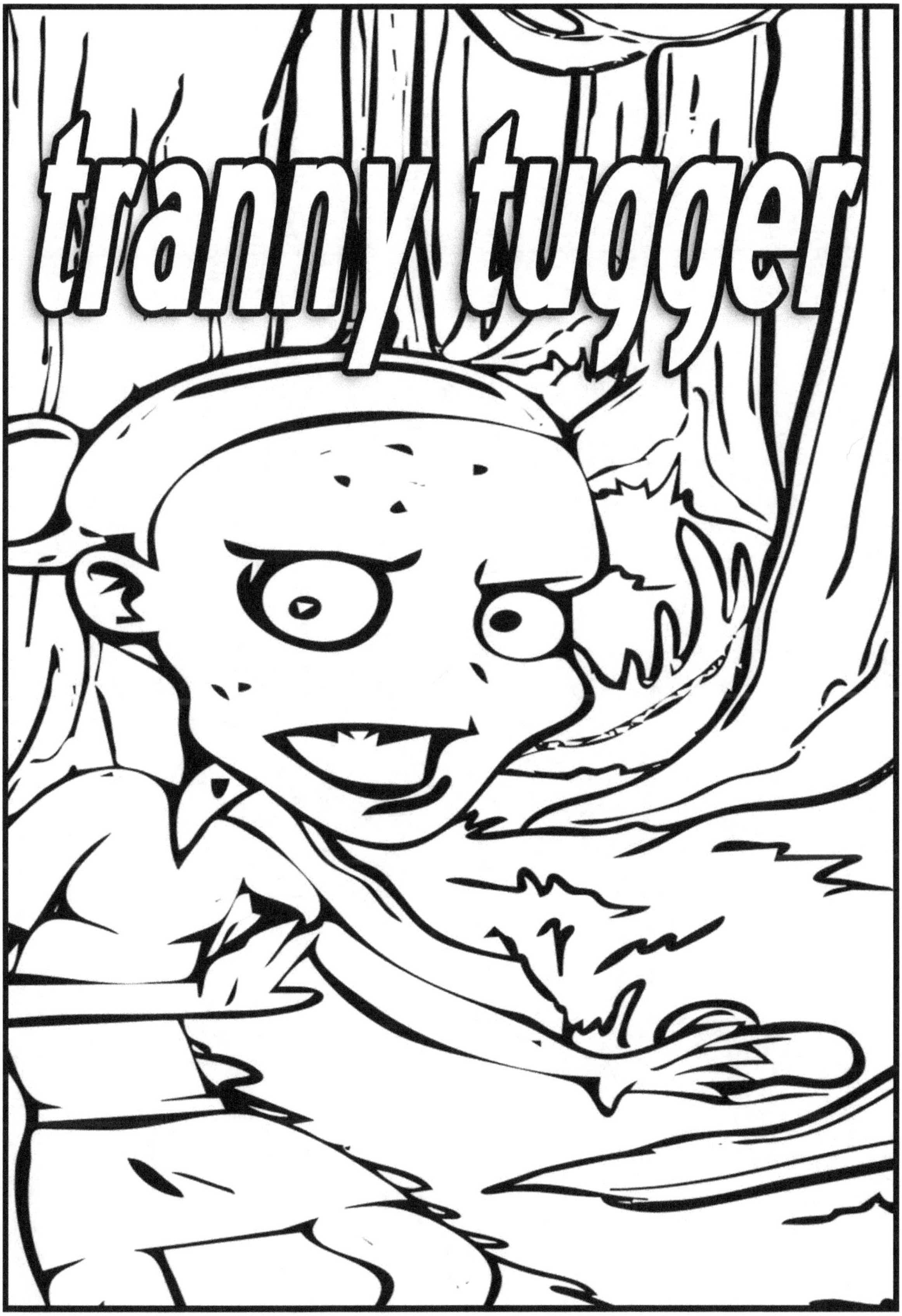
tranny tugger

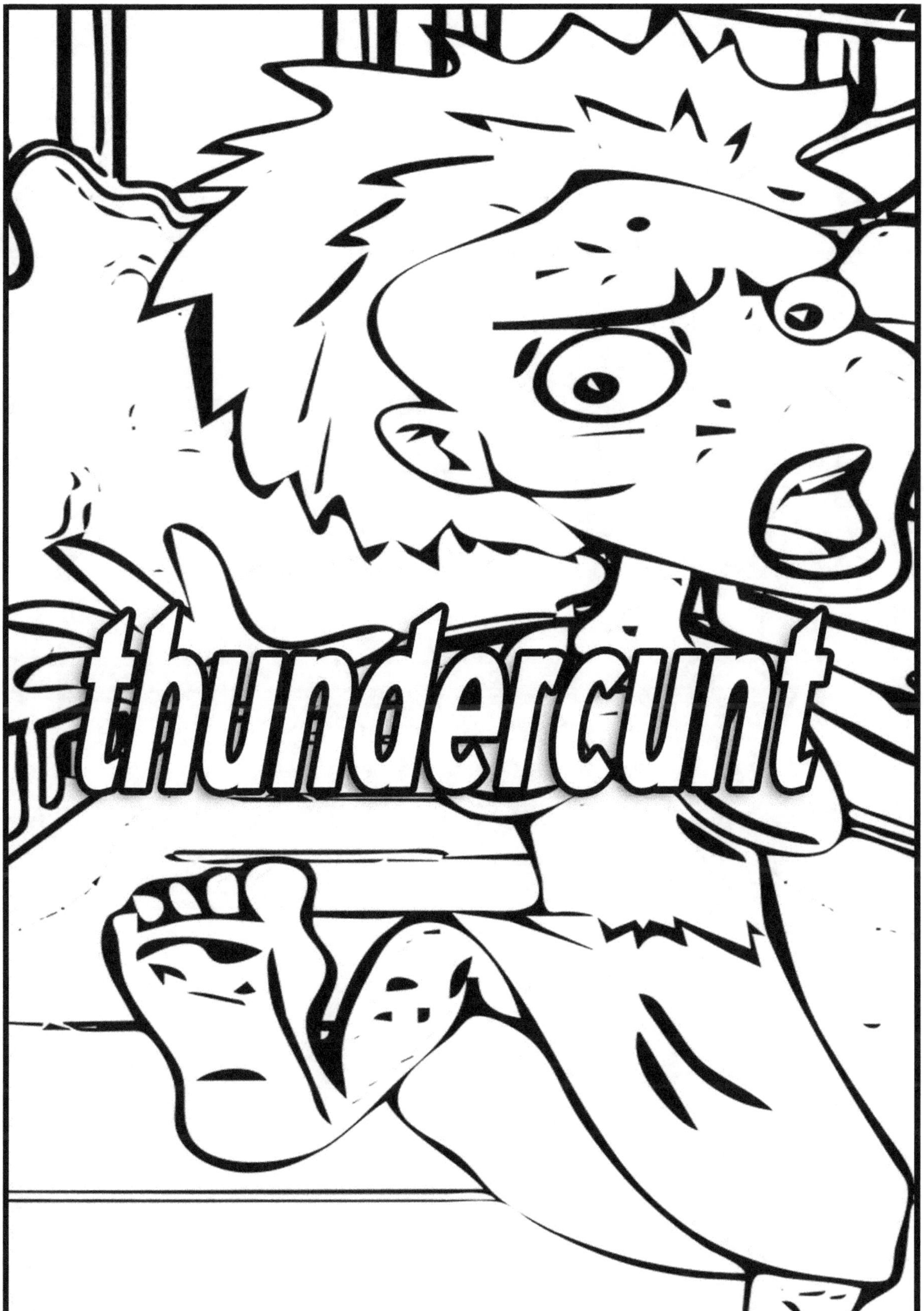
thundercunt

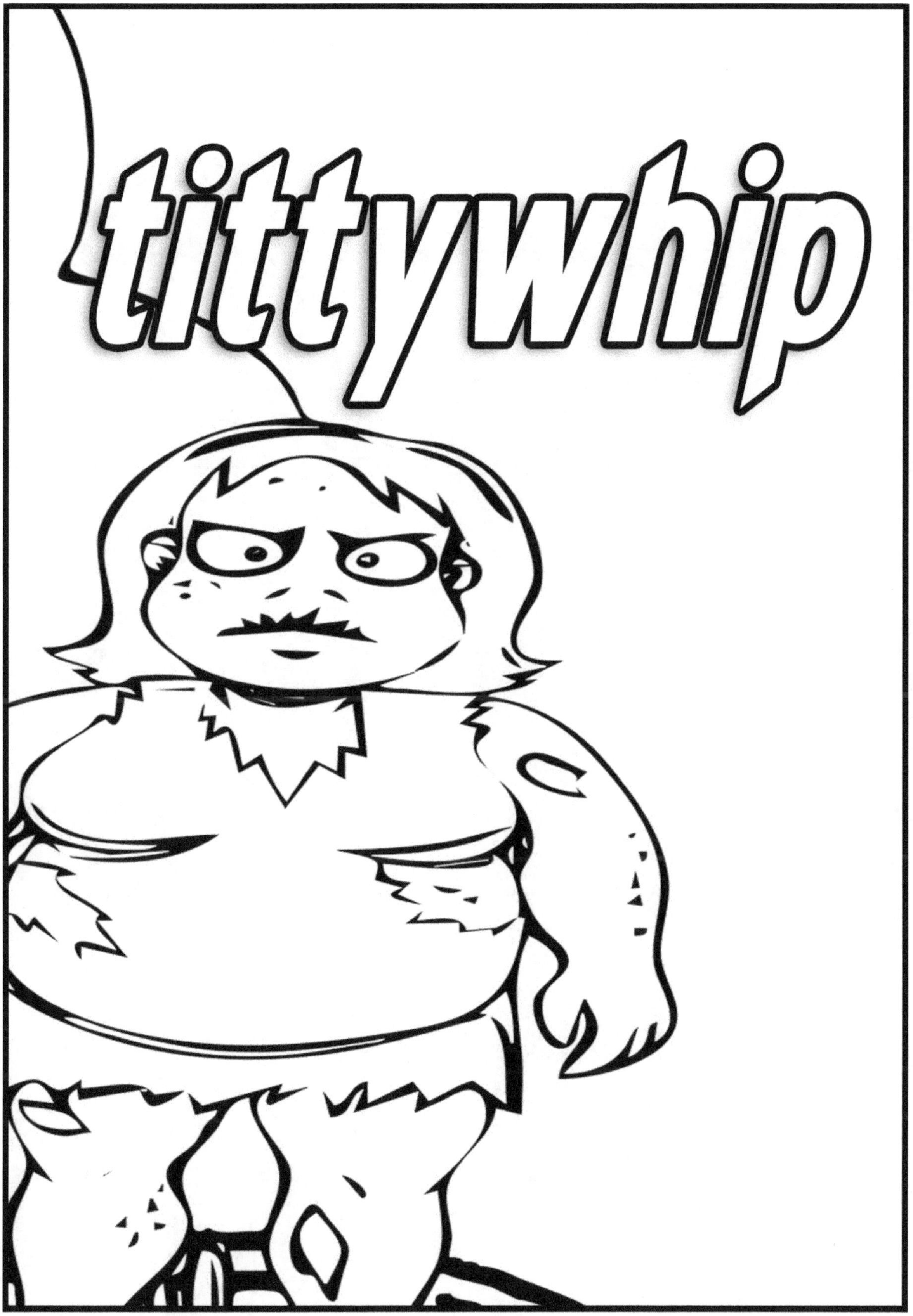
tittywhip

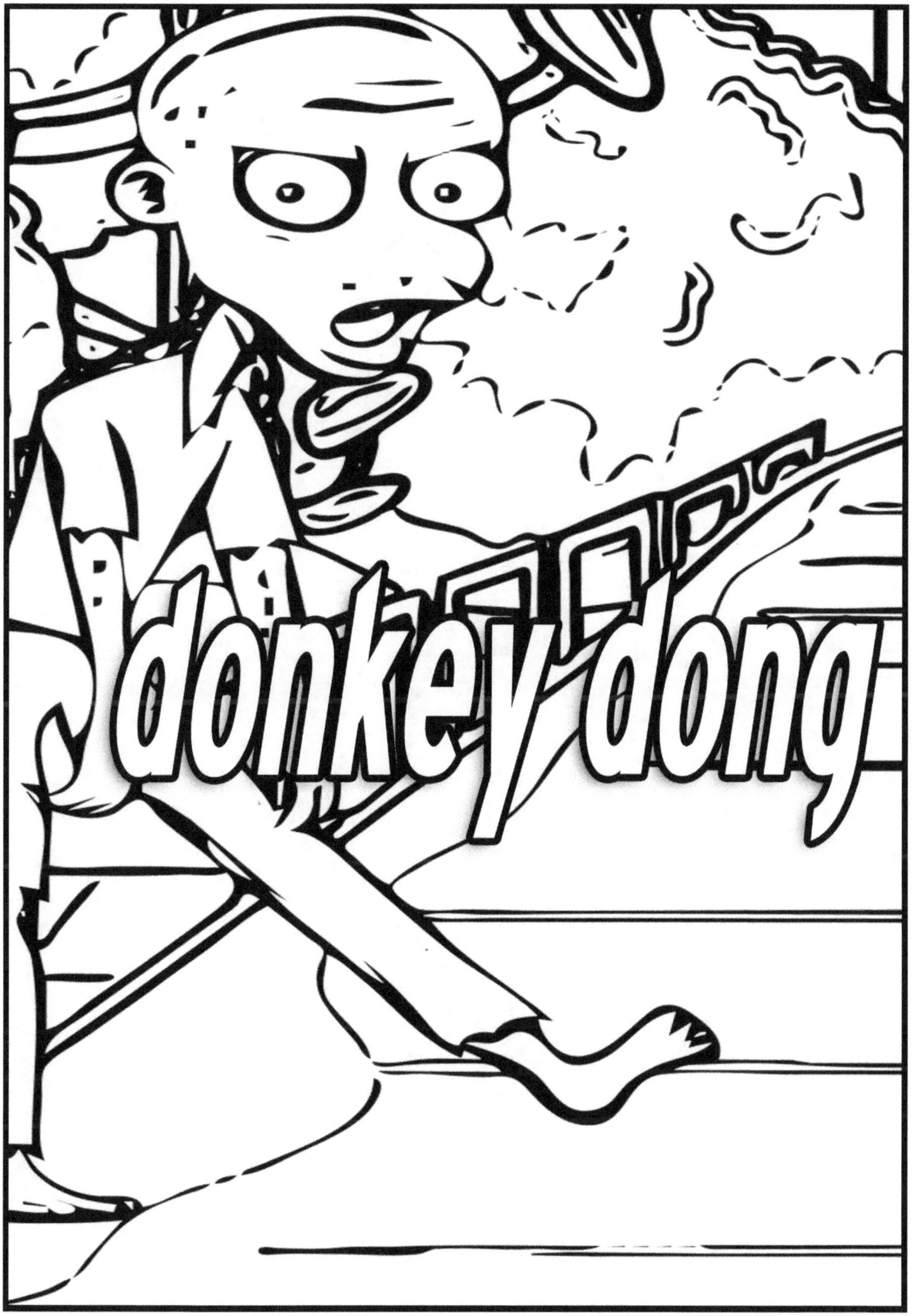
donkey dong

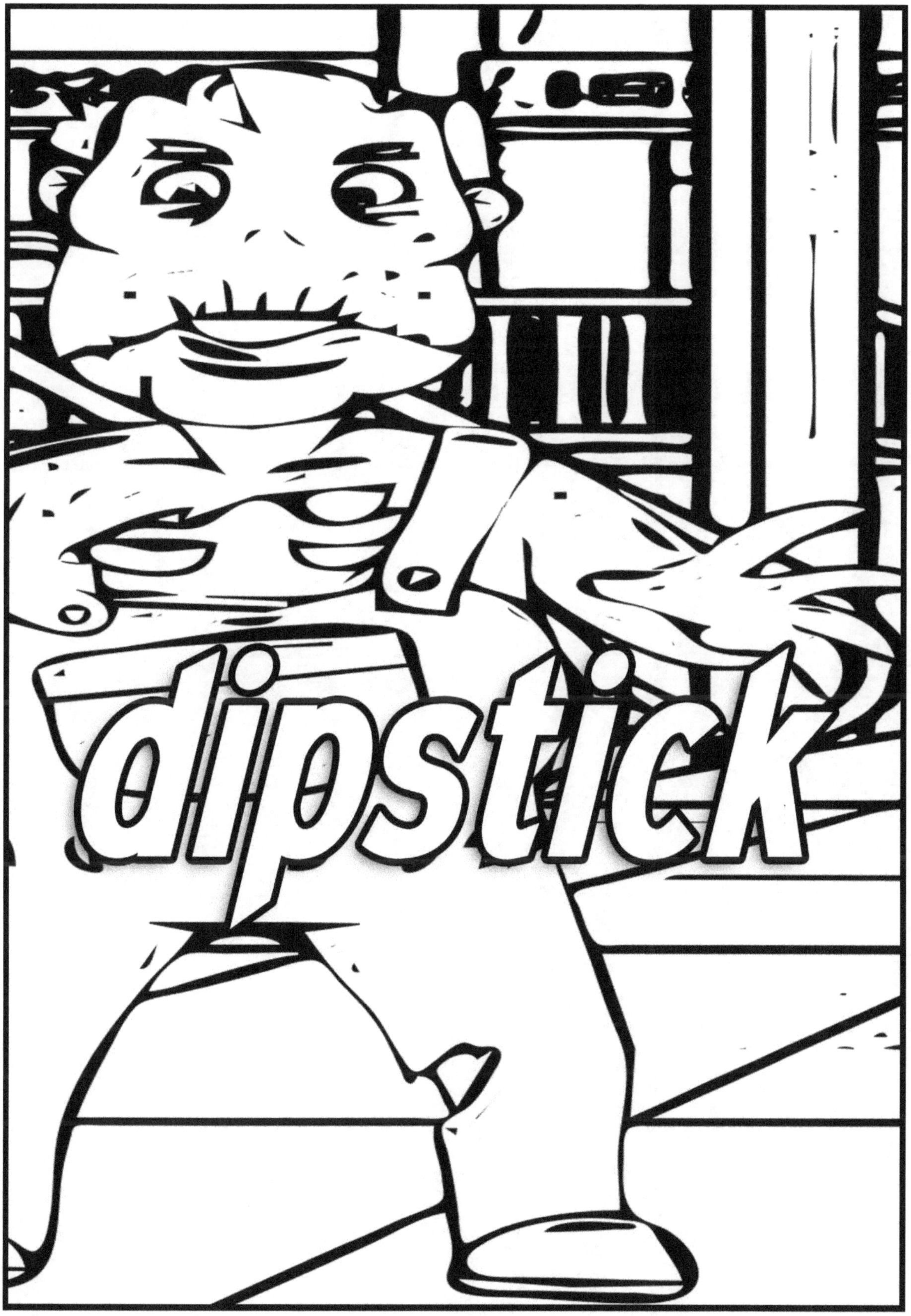
dipstick

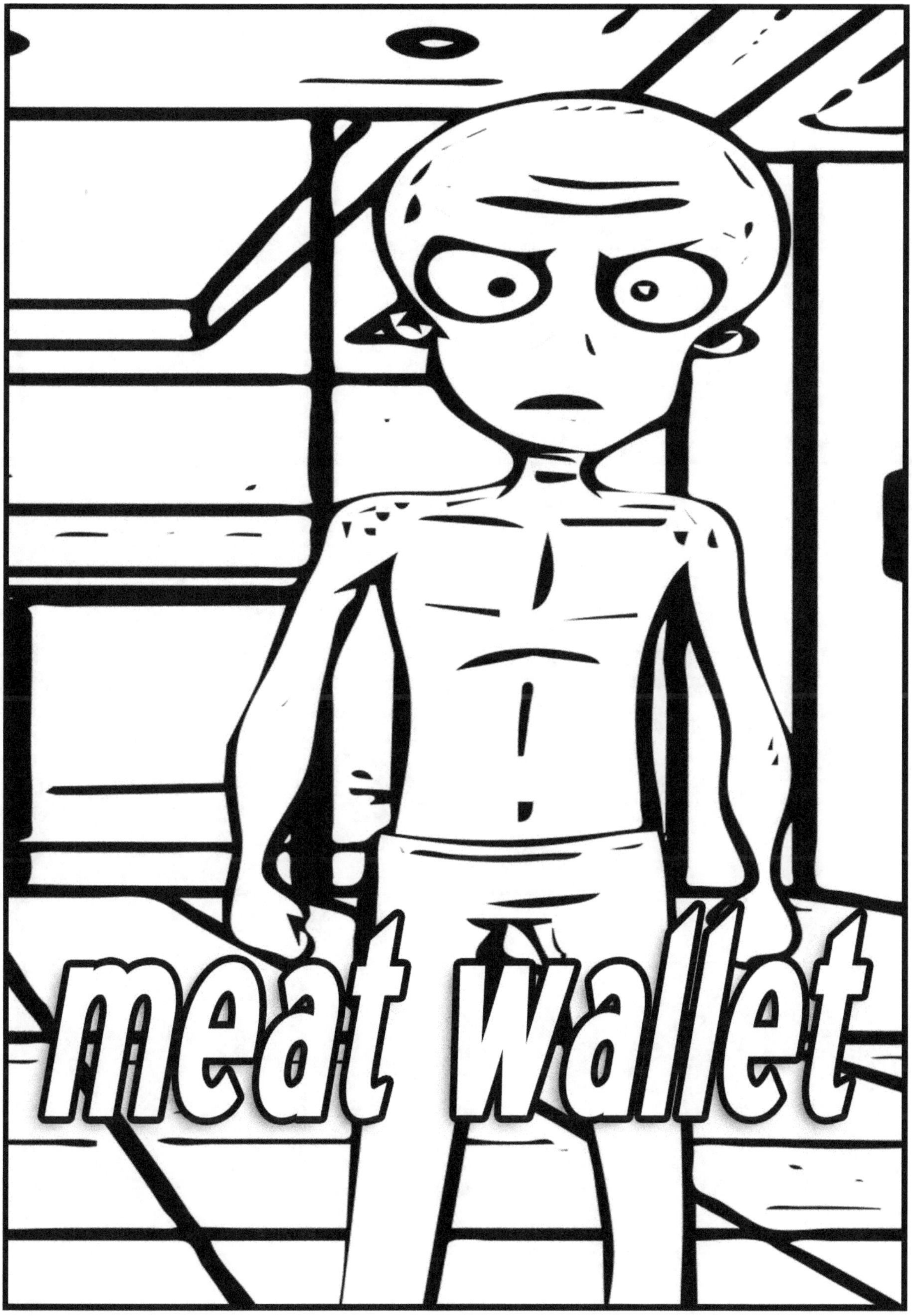
meat wallet

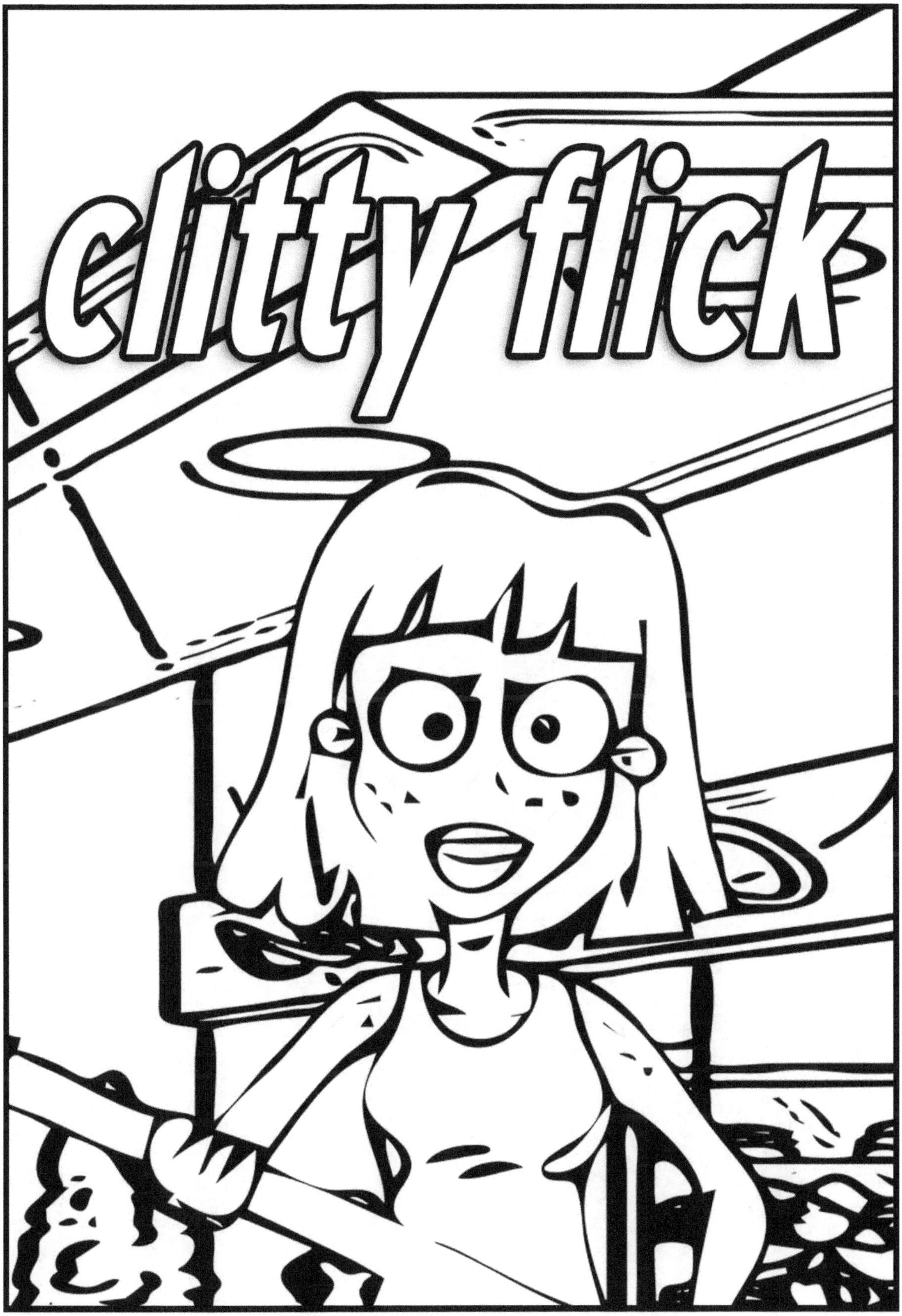
clitty flick

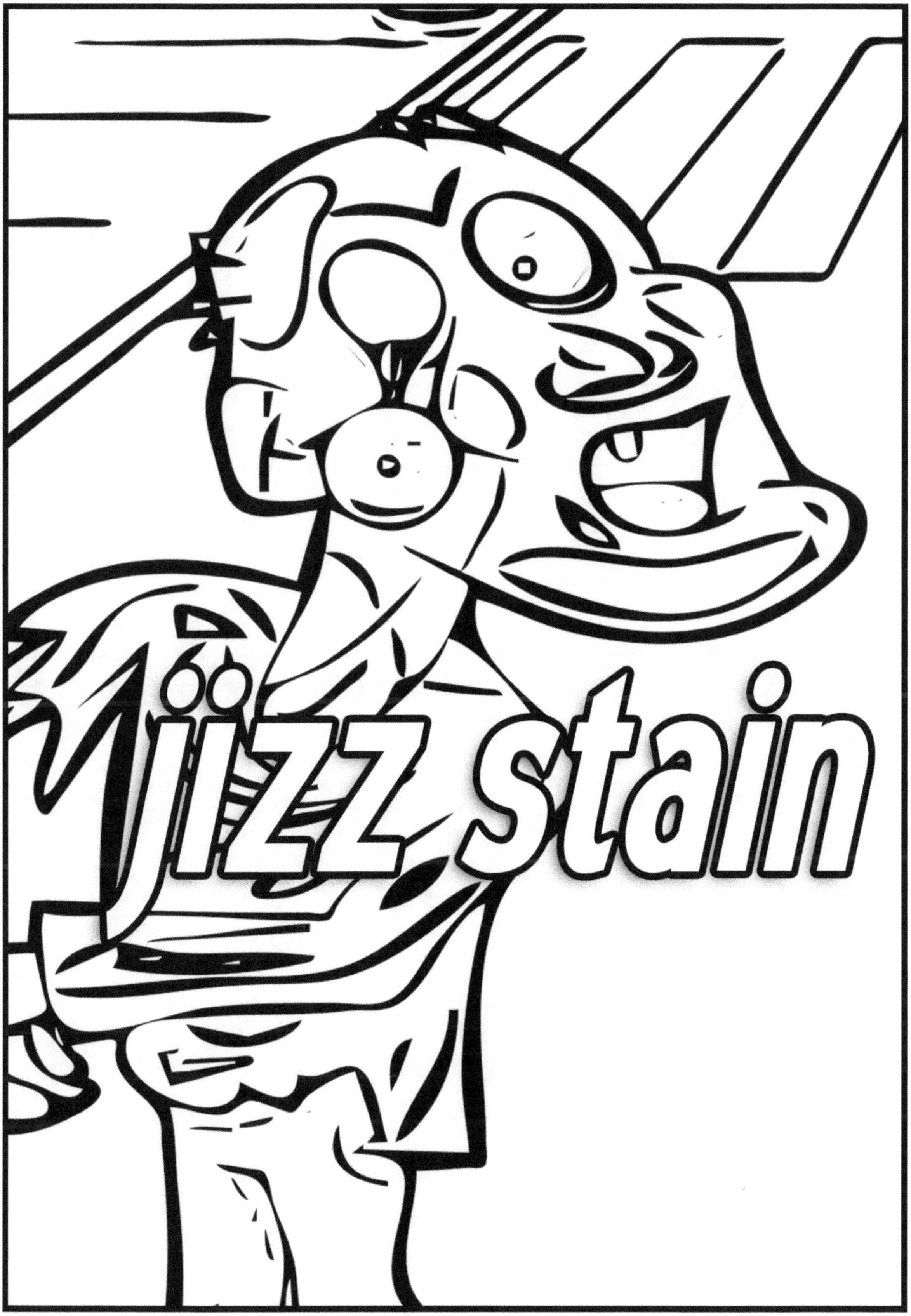
jïzz stain

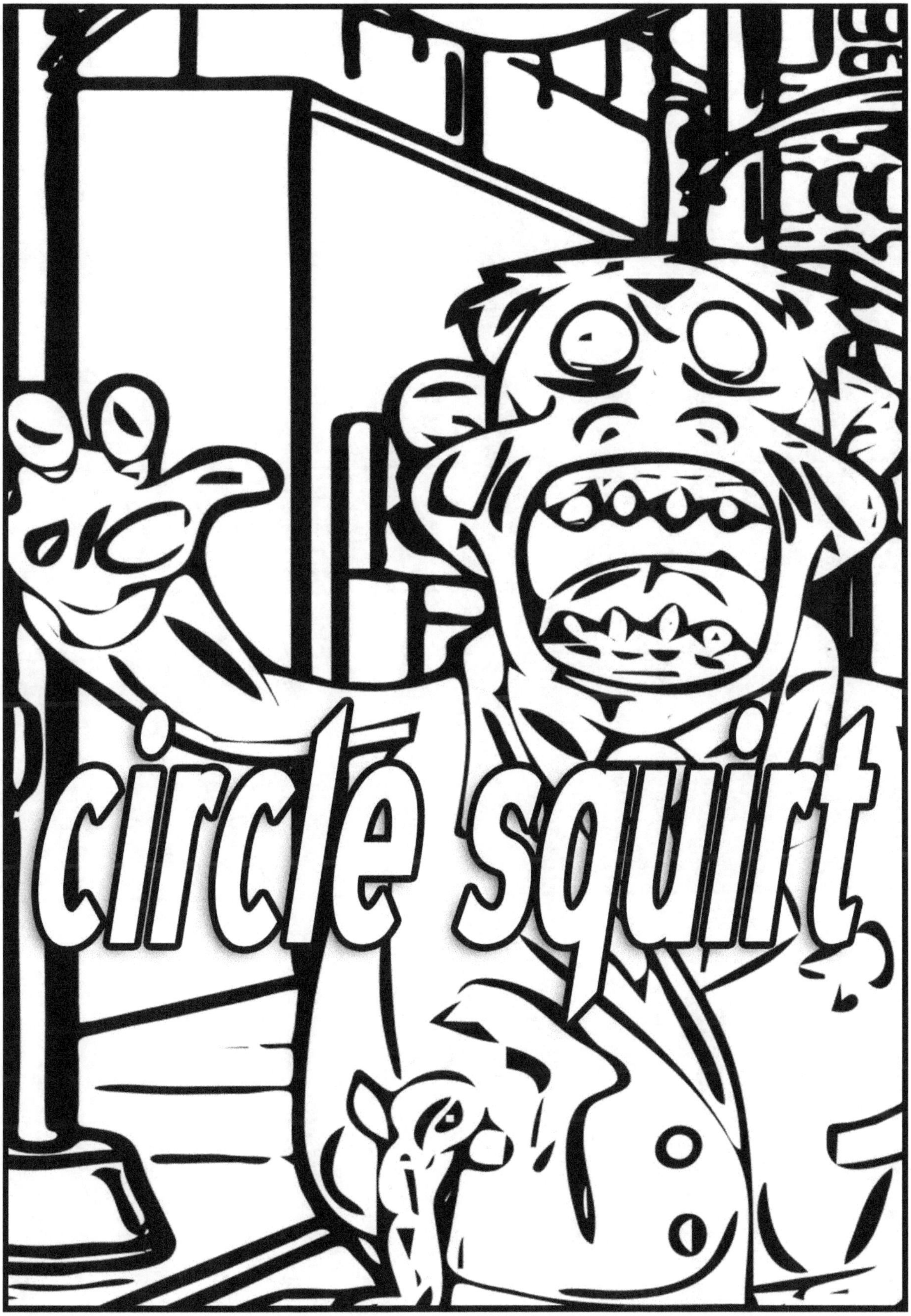
circle squirt

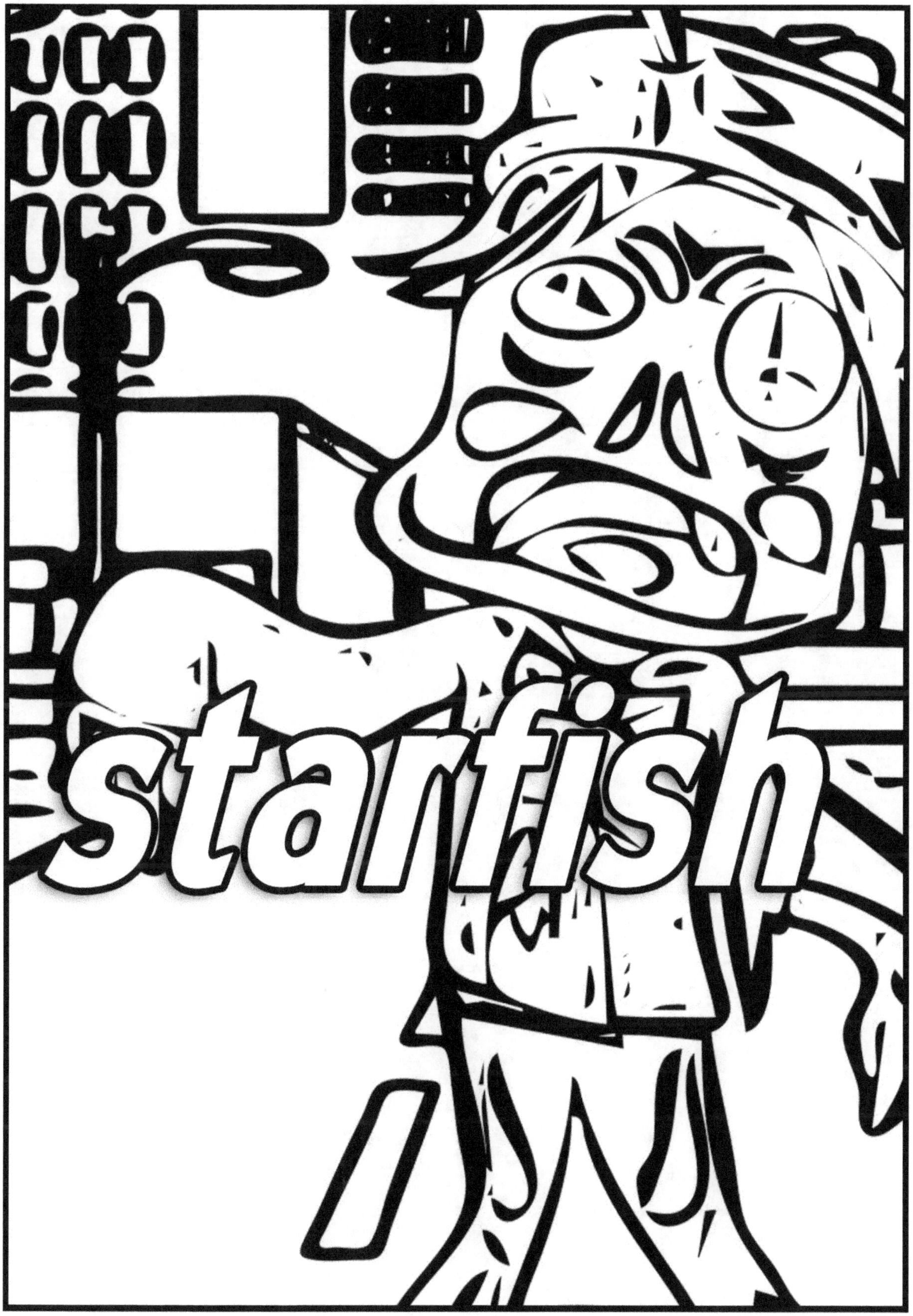
starfish

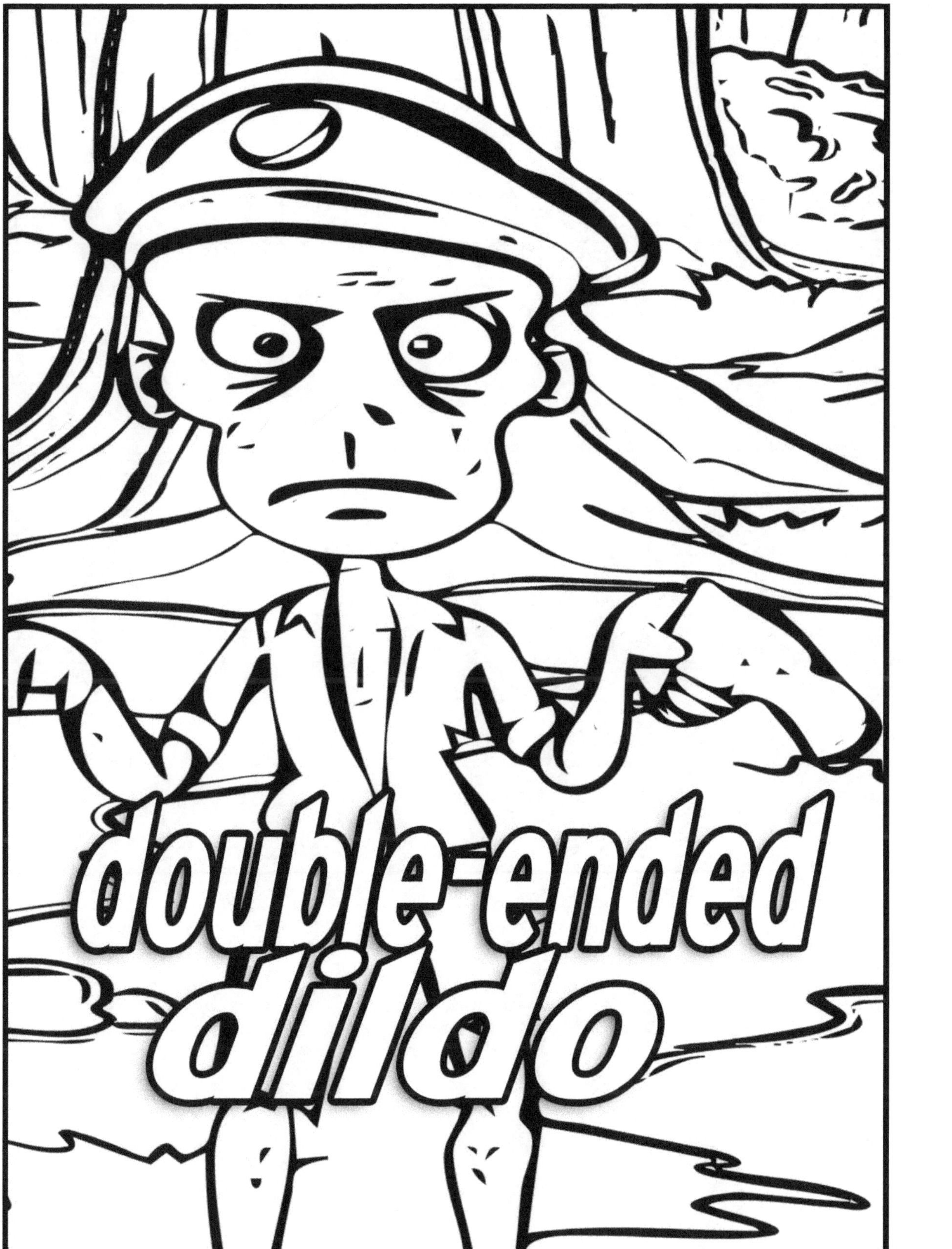
double-ended
dildo

www.ingramcontent.com/pod-product-compliance
Lightning Source LLC
Chambersburg PA
CBHW080612190526
45169CB00007B/2981